What Is the Metaverse?

A Beginner's Guide to Virtual Worlds, Digital Real Estate, and the Future of the Internet

By Joe Correa

Published by Live Stronger Faster

This book is for educational and informational purposes only. The author and publisher are not engaged in rendering legal, financial, or other professional advice. Readers should consult a qualified professional before making any financial decisions.

First Edition

Table of Contents

Overview

Imagine walking into a digital world where you can own property, run a business, attend concerts, design fashion, and even earn income — all without leaving your home. That's not a sci-fi dream anymore; it's the Metaverse. This evolving digital universe represents the next major evolution of the internet — a 3D, interactive, immersive space powered by blockchain, artificial intelligence, and virtual reality.

The term *"Metaverse"* might sound futuristic, but it's already here in many forms — from gaming worlds like Roblox and Fortnite to decentralized platforms like Decentraland and The Sandbox. In the simplest terms, the Metaverse is a network of interconnected virtual spaces where people can socialize, work, play, and build economies. It's the digital parallel of our physical world — only limited by imagination.

The concept became mainstream when major tech giants like Meta (formerly Facebook), Microsoft, and Apple began investing billions to build the next internet frontier. But beyond the headlines and hype, the Metaverse is more than virtual reality headsets and avatars — it's about redefining how humans connect, collaborate, and create value online. It's the beginning of an entirely new digital economy where ownership, identity, and creativity merge seamlessly through blockchain and Web3 technologies.

For beginners, the Metaverse can feel overwhelming. You might wonder: *How do I enter these worlds? What can I actually do there? Can I make money?* This audiobook answers all those questions and more. You'll learn how the Metaverse works, who's building it, and how you can participate — even if you have no tech skills or coding experience.

Understanding the Metaverse today is like learning about the internet in the 1990s — early adopters stand to benefit the most. Whether you're a student, investor, entrepreneur, or creative thinker, this is your opportunity to get ahead of a transformation that will reshape how the world lives, learns, and earns.

By the end of this book, you'll understand the foundations of the Metaverse, the technologies behind it, and why it's being called *the next trillion-dollar economy*. The journey begins with curiosity — and a willingness to explore this brave new digital world. Let's step inside.

Chapter 1

The Birth of a New Digital Universe

The Metaverse didn't appear overnight. Its roots stretch back decades, beginning with the earliest forms of online connectivity. To truly understand what's coming, you must first grasp how we got here.

From the Internet to Immersion

The first version of the internet, now known as *Web 1.0*, was static — users could only read what others published. Then came *Web 2.0*, the social-media era that allowed people to create, share, and interact. It democratized communication but centralized power in the hands of large platforms like Facebook, YouTube, and Twitter. The *Metaverse* represents the next stage — *Web 3.0* — where interaction becomes immersive and ownership shifts to users themselves through blockchain technology.

The Building Blocks of the Metaverse

1. **Virtual Reality (VR)** — Headsets and 3D environments immerse users fully inside digital spaces.

2. **Augmented Reality (AR)** — Digital layers that enhance the real world, merging physical and virtual

experiences.

3. **Blockchain & Cryptocurrency** – The foundation of digital ownership; NFTs and tokens prove who owns land, assets, and identities inside these worlds.

4. **Artificial Intelligence (AI)** – Creates responsive environments and intelligent NPCs (non-player characters).

5. **Interoperability** – The ability to move identities, avatars, and assets between different virtual worlds.

Each of these technologies contributes to a shared universe that exists beyond any single company's control.

The Visionaries Who Started It All

The term *"Metaverse"* was first coined by author Neal Stephenson in his 1992 novel *Snow Crash*. His fictional vision of avatars walking through virtual streets became a template for what companies now strive to build. Later, games like *Second Life* and *Minecraft* turned parts of that fiction into interactive reality. Today, projects such as *Decentraland, The Sandbox, Meta Horizon Worlds*, and *Roblox* are evolving it into a living, breathing ecosystem.

Why Ownership Matters

Traditional digital experiences belong to the platforms that host them. In the Metaverse, thanks to blockchain, users *own* their digital property. Whether it's a plot of land, a piece of clothing for an avatar, or an NFT artwork, ownership is recorded on a decentralized ledger. This creates an entirely new economy — one where value can be created, traded, and monetized across borders instantly.

Economic and Social Potential

The Metaverse isn't limited to gaming. Businesses can hold virtual meetings, artists can host concerts, teachers can run immersive classrooms, and real-estate developers can design entire cities that exist purely online. Global banks, fashion brands, and entertainment companies are investing heavily in this frontier because it unlocks a borderless economy worth trillions.

The Beginner's Mindset

To navigate this transformation, curiosity is your greatest asset. Don't worry about mastering every technical detail. Instead, learn the principles of decentralization, explore virtual platforms, and experiment. Just as early YouTubers built empires with simple videos, early Metaverse pioneers are laying the foundation for tomorrow's digital nations.

The Metaverse isn't the end of the internet — it's its rebirth. It transforms screens into worlds, profiles into people, and clicks into experiences. Understanding this shift today will place you years ahead of the crowd.

"Through the Digital Door"

Lena adjusted her headset nervously. The sleek black visor covered her eyes as a glowing message appeared: *"Welcome to Horizon City — Enter?"* She hesitated, took a deep breath, and whispered, "Yes."

In an instant, her living room faded. The sound of birds, city chatter, and distant music surrounded her. She stood in a plaza lined with floating billboards, glass towers, and avatars from every corner of the world. Some wore elegant suits, others dressed as dragons or robots. A neon-blue sign above her blinked: *"Trade Center District →."*

Lena had read about the Metaverse for months but never imagined it could feel *this real.* A friendly avatar approached — a man wearing virtual jeans and a glowing badge that read *GuideBot XR*. "First time?" he asked with a smile.

"Is it that obvious?" she replied, laughing nervously. "Everyone's a newbie once. Follow me — I'll show you where people buy land and build shops."

They walked toward a floating elevator that rose above the cityscape. Below, Lena saw digital billboards advertising NFT art galleries and concert arenas. In the distance, holographic signs displayed cryptocurrency exchange rates and rental prices for virtual apartments.

"Wait, people actually pay for this land?" she asked.

"Of course," said XR. "Every plot is on the blockchain — totally owned by its buyer. Some flipped properties for hundreds of thousands. Others host games or virtual offices. The city runs on smart contracts, so no middlemen, no borders."

Lena's curiosity burned brighter. She stepped off the elevator into an open terrace filled with avatars networking and pitching ideas. A woman wearing a futuristic jacket handed her a digital business card that materialized mid-air: *'Virtual Architect — Designing Spaces for Brands and Creators.'*

For the first time, Lena realized she wasn't just witnessing technology — she was witnessing a civilization forming from code. People here weren't escaping reality; they were *rebuilding it.*

As she wandered through the district, she found an art gallery where the walls shimmered with NFT paintings. Each piece displayed its creator's wallet address and market value. The gallery owner, a teenager from Brazil, proudly said, "I opened this store last year. I've sold forty-two NFTs — enough to pay my college tuition."

That night, when Lena logged off, her living room reappeared. The contrast felt surreal. Yet something inside her had shifted. She no longer saw the Metaverse as fantasy but as the next evolution of human experience — a realm where imagination could finally take physical form.

Lena removed her headset and whispered, "This isn't a game. It's the beginning of something huge."

Chapter 2

Understanding Virtual Worlds

To truly understand the Metaverse, you must first grasp the concept of **virtual worlds** — digital environments where people live, work, and play through avatars and digital identities. These worlds form the foundation of everything we call "the Metaverse."

The Anatomy of a Virtual World

Every virtual world — whether it's *Roblox*, *Decentraland*, *The Sandbox*, or *Horizon Worlds* — shares a few fundamental characteristics:

1. **Persistent Digital Space:** The world continues to exist and evolve even when you log off. Unlike traditional video games, virtual worlds persist independently of individual players.

2. **Social Interaction:** Communication is central. Avatars can talk, trade, collaborate, or attend events in real time. Communities are built around shared interests, brands, and creative projects.

3. **Economy and Ownership:** Virtual worlds have functioning economies where digital goods hold value.

Users can buy land, fashion, or services using native tokens or cryptocurrencies. Ownership is verified through blockchain, allowing resale, rental, and passive income opportunities.

4. **Creativity and Contribution:** Users are not just consumers but *creators*. Virtual architects, designers, musicians, and educators shape these worlds by building interactive spaces and experiences.

5. **Interoperability:** The next evolution of virtual worlds is interoperability — the ability to move assets, currency, and identity across different platforms seamlessly. In a truly connected Metaverse, your avatar could attend a meeting in *Horizon Worlds*, play a game in *The Sandbox*, and then shop in *Decentraland* without losing identity or possessions.

How Virtual Worlds Differ from Traditional Games

Although gaming paved the way for 3D digital environments, the Metaverse represents a leap beyond entertainment. In gaming, goals and storylines are defined by developers. In the Metaverse, *you* define your own objectives. You might start a business, host a concert, or teach a class — actions that generate real income. The focus is on creativity, commerce, and community rather than competition.

The New Digital Citizenship

Your *avatar* becomes your identity — a visual representation of who you are or wish to be. It's how you express personality, profession, and status. In virtual worlds, reputation is currency. The more value you bring to others, the more influence and opportunity you attract.

Soon, resumes may include virtual achievements — "Built a top-rated education hub in Decentraland" or "Managed a digital real-estate agency in The Sandbox." Companies are already hiring creators who understand digital-world dynamics.

The Emotional Connection

Humans crave immersion and connection. The Metaverse satisfies both by blending imagination with reality. Meeting someone's avatar feels surprisingly real because gestures, tone, and shared activities simulate in-person experience. Psychologically, the brain treats these virtual interactions as genuine social experiences.

Practical Steps to Explore Virtual Worlds

1. **Create a Wallet:** You'll need a crypto wallet (like MetaMask) to own land, NFTs, or digital currency.

2. **Pick a Platform:** Start free — explore *Roblox, Spatial,* or *Horizon Worlds.*

3. **Customize Your Avatar:** Express your personality; your digital look matters.

4. **Join a Community:** Participate in meetups or Discord groups to learn from others.

5. **Attend Events:** Concerts, classes, and conferences are great entry points.

Virtual worlds are the new frontier — part playground, part marketplace, part university. Whether you're an artist, entrepreneur, or explorer, these worlds offer a canvas to experiment, collaborate, and profit.

"The Virtual Architect"

Arjun was an architect in Mumbai, known for designing eco-friendly homes that blended nature and technology. When the pandemic hit, construction halted. Clients disappeared. One sleepless night, scrolling through YouTube, he stumbled upon a video titled *"Building in the Metaverse — How Architects Are Making a Fortune Online."*

Curious, he clicked. The video showed creators designing virtual museums, offices, and concert halls for companies inside *The Sandbox*. They weren't just designing — they were *selling* their creations as NFTs. Arjun's heart raced. "Could I design buildings for a world that doesn't physically exist?" he whispered.

The next day, he downloaded *Decentraland's Builder* tool. At first, everything felt foreign — the interface, the block-based layout, the avatars walking by. But the creative freedom was intoxicating. No gravity, no permits, no construction costs. Just imagination.

He started by building a glass dome structure — a floating design he could never have achieved in real life. He added waterfalls, holographic trees, and sky bridges that connected to virtual stores. Within a week, he uploaded his design to the marketplace.

A message popped up a few days later: *"Your design has been purchased for 2 ETH."* He stared at the screen in disbelief. It was more than his monthly salary.

Encouraged, Arjun joined Metaverse communities, met digital fashion designers, NFT artists, and even real-estate investors. They spoke a new language — of "minting," "staking," and "decentralized land." But he adapted quickly. His skills from the physical world gave him an advantage. Months later, he launched *ArjunVR Studio*, offering virtual architecture for global clients. A famous DJ hired him to build an interactive nightclub that reacted to music frequencies. Another client commissioned a meditation temple floating above a digital ocean.

One evening, Arjun logged in to show a client around his new creation — an eco-metropolis powered by renewable "energy tokens." As he walked his avatar through the glowing streets, he smiled. The skyline reflected not glass or steel but *possibility*.

For the first time, Arjun realized he was no longer just an architect of buildings. He was an architect of worlds. The Metaverse had not replaced his career — it had *expanded* it beyond imagination.

Chapter 3

How the Metaverse Works: The Technology Behind the Magic

The Metaverse may feel like fantasy when you're inside it, but underneath the visual wonder lies a powerful fusion of technologies working together in real time. Understanding these layers is essential for anyone who wants to build, invest, or innovate within this new digital frontier.

1 — The Foundation: Web 3.0 and Blockchain

At its core, the Metaverse depends on **blockchain** — a distributed digital ledger that records ownership, identity, and transactions without a central authority. Each "block" stores verified data, ensuring transparency and security.

Blockchain enables true **digital property rights**. When you buy land, mint an NFT, or earn crypto in a virtual world, the proof of ownership is recorded on-chain and cannot be altered. This decentralization shifts control away from corporations toward users, making the Metaverse an open ecosystem instead of a walled garden.

2 — Smart Contracts and Digital Economies

Smart contracts are self-executing programs stored on the blockchain that automatically enforce rules and payments. For example, if a virtual concert sells 500 tickets, a smart contract can instantly distribute revenue among artists, venue owners, and affiliates.

This automation builds trust and efficiency into the Metaverse economy. It eliminates middlemen, reduces fraud, and allows micro-transactions that make small-scale commerce viable — from renting a digital billboard for 24 hours to selling a single pixel of virtual art.

3 — 3D Engines and World-Building Frameworks

Behind every immersive experience are powerful **3D engines** such as Unreal Engine 5, Unity, and Babylon.js. These render environments, physics, lighting, and animation. The level of realism achieved today rivals blockbuster films, yet runs smoothly on home devices and even in browsers.

These engines also allow creators to script behavior: doors that open when approached, avatars that react to gestures, economies that fluctuate based on supply and demand. The result is a living, responsive digital world.

4 — Virtual Reality (VR) and Augmented Reality (AR)

VR headsets like Meta Quest 3 or Apple Vision Pro immerse users fully inside digital space, tracking motion and perspective for natural interaction. AR, on the other hand, overlays virtual content onto the physical world — think virtual furniture previews or wearable heads-up displays.

Together, VR and AR create what experts call **"extended reality" (XR)** — the seamless blend of real and digital dimensions that defines the Metaverse experience.

5 — Artificial Intelligence and Automation

AI powers nearly everything unseen: real-time translation, voice recognition, emotion analysis, and dynamic environment creation. Non-player characters (NPCs) can respond intelligently to conversations. AI can also generate 3D objects, buildings, or entire worlds in seconds, drastically lowering entry barriers for new creators.

6 — Interoperability and Digital Identity

The ultimate vision of the Metaverse is **interoperability** — the ability to carry your avatar, assets, and reputation across multiple worlds. Standards such as Open Metaverse Alliance and W3C Decentralized Identifiers (DIDs) aim to make this possible.

Instead of dozens of logins and disconnected inventories, your single digital identity will one day serve as your passport to every virtual destination.

7 — The Future Stack: 5G, Edge Computing & Cloud Infrastructure

Fast, low-latency connections are essential. 5G and edge computing bring servers closer to users, enabling massive multiplayer environments with instant synchronization. Cloud-based rendering means even mobile devices can access rich, high-fidelity worlds without high-end hardware.

Putting It All Together

When you step into the Metaverse, these technologies combine in milliseconds. Your headset connects to a 3D engine hosted in the cloud. Blockchain verifies your identity and assets. Smart contracts execute transactions. AI fills in details. Edge servers minimize lag. The result feels magical — but it's pure engineering mastery woven into an experience that feels human.

The Metaverse isn't just "virtual reality." It's the internet reborn — interactive, intelligent, and owned by its users.

"Behind the Code"

Maya had always been fascinated by worlds that didn't exist. As a teenager she built Minecraft castles; as an adult, she designed 3D models for architecture firms in London. Yet something felt incomplete. She wanted to create spaces people could *live* in, not just view on a screen.

One evening, while watching a livestream about The Sandbox, she saw a headline scroll across the chat: *"Hiring World Builders — Experience with Unity preferred."* Her heart skipped. She clicked the link, uploaded her portfolio, and within a week she was accepted as a junior designer for Metaverse Labs, a startup constructing virtual campuses for universities worldwide.

Her first day on the project was nothing like she imagined. Instead of cranes and cement, there were code windows and polygons. A senior engineer named Leo explained, "Think of the blockchain as the city's land registry. Every plot, building, or asset you create is registered on it forever."

He showed her how a smart contract worked: lines of code that automatically paid royalties every time a digital textbook was sold inside their campus. "No middlemen," he smiled. "Just math and trust." Maya spent nights experimenting with Unreal Engine 5. She watched the sun rise through the glass windows of her real apartment while simultaneously adjusting the lighting of a virtual sunrise in her digital one. Each tweak changed how students would feel inside her classroom simulation — brighter hues for energy, softer tones for focus.

Weeks later, she put on her VR headset and walked into the university's virtual library for the first time. AI-driven assistants greeted her: avatars that could answer questions in twenty languages. Students from Brazil, Nigeria, and Japan wandered the aisles together, discussing projects as holographic diagrams floated above their desks.

One student paused to admire a book display. When he purchased a digital copy, Maya saw the transaction execute in real time on the blockchain dashboard — instant royalties, no delay, no intermediary.

Later, Leo joined her for a walk through the campus gardens. "Do you realize," he said, "what you're seeing is millions of lines of code coordinating through AI and 5G to make you believe in a world that isn't there — yet feels as real as this conversation?"

Maya nodded. For the first time, she understood that the Metaverse wasn't just graphics or gadgets. It was a living network of technologies woven together to create a new dimension of human experience. As she watched the digital sky glow above her creation, she smiled and whispered, “This is the magic behind the code.”

Chapter 4

The Economy of the Metaverse: Earning and Spending in Virtual Worlds

The Metaverse isn't just a playground of imagination — it's a functioning economy. Every digital world has its own marketplace, currency, and set of opportunities that mirror, and often surpass, real-world systems. Understanding how value flows in this environment is the key to turning participation into profit.

1 — Digital Currency and Value Exchange

Most virtual worlds run on cryptocurrencies or native tokens that serve as their economic backbone. *Decentraland* uses MANA; *The Sandbox* uses SAND; *Axie Infinity* uses AXS. These tokens are traded on global exchanges just like Bitcoin or Ethereum, giving virtual assets real-world liquidity.

When users purchase digital land, clothing, art, or services, transactions are recorded on the blockchain. Because of this, virtual economies function independently of traditional banking systems — anyone with an internet connection can participate.

2 — The Rise of Digital Ownership

Ownership is what differentiates the Metaverse from previous online worlds. In Web 2.0 games, everything belonged to the platform; in Web 3.0 worlds, ownership is decentralized and verifiable. You truly *own* your avatar's jacket, your art gallery, or your private island.

This changes behavior. When people own digital property, they treat it as an investment. They renovate, rent, trade, and protect it, just as they would real real estate.

3 — Earning Income in the Metaverse

There are countless ways to generate income in this economy:

- **Virtual Real Estate:** Buy land in early-stage worlds and sell or rent it later.
- **Digital Design:** Create wearables, furniture, or architecture for others.
- **Entertainment:** Host concerts, comedy shows, or immersive experiences with paid admission.
- **Education:** Build training centers, workshops, and tutoring spaces.

- **Play-to-Earn Games:** Earn tokens by completing tasks or quests.
- **Advertising:** Lease your virtual property for brand placements.

Entrepreneurs are already making full-time incomes through these channels, and entire agencies now specialize in virtual-world marketing, construction, and events.

4 — Spending and Circulation of Wealth

Spending is as important as earning. Users reinvest their earnings into better land parcels, upgraded avatars, or collectible NFTs. Just like real economies, this circulation drives growth. Brands enter these ecosystems to sell products, host experiences, and reward loyalty through digital tokens.

In many platforms, you can instantly convert earnings into fiat currency or stake them to earn passive yield, creating a hybrid between investing and gameplay.

5 — The Role of NFTs

Non-fungible tokens (NFTs) act as digital certificates of authenticity. Every asset — a painting, a house, a pair of shoes — can be tokenized and resold with royalties automatically returning to the creator. This has transformed how artists, musicians, and developers earn ongoing income.

6 — Challenges and Cautions

Like any emerging market, the Metaverse economy has risks: volatility, scams, and speculative bubbles. Successful participants treat it like a business — researching projects, tracking communities, and diversifying holdings.

The lesson: **approach with curiosity but operate with discipline.** The Metaverse rewards innovation but punishes recklessness.

7 — The Future of Work and Wealth

As virtual worlds mature, more people will earn their living entirely online — as virtual architects, event producers, or asset traders. The lines between "job" and "game" will blur. Early adopters who understand this shift are positioning themselves to become the landlords, educators, and entrepreneurs of the new digital frontier.

The Metaverse is no longer a fantasy economy. It's a borderless marketplace where creativity, attention, and innovation are the new forms of capital.

"The Digital Merchant"

Ethan used to run a small T-shirt shop on a side street in Los Angeles. Sales were steady but uninspiring, and when lockdowns hit, his business nearly collapsed. One night, scrolling through social media, he saw a post about *The Sandbox*: "Artists earning six-figure incomes selling virtual wearables."

He laughed at first. "Who buys clothes they can't touch?" But curiosity won. He downloaded the creation tool, watched tutorials, and designed a neon-blue jacket with animated circuitry running through its sleeves. It took him two days to get the texture right, another two to mint it as an NFT.

Within a week, the jacket sold for 0.6 ETH. Someone even posted a screenshot of their avatar wearing it at a Metaverse fashion event. That image went viral. Orders poured in.

Ethan rebranded himself as *MetaThreadz*, a digital-only fashion house. His living room became his studio; his models were avatars from around the world. Instead of worrying about fabric costs or shipping delays, he focused on design and storytelling. Each collection came with unlockable perks — entry to virtual concerts or exclusive meetups. Soon he hired a small team of creators from Brazil, Japan, and Nigeria. They met daily inside *Spatial*, a sleek VR workspace surrounded by floating sketches. Their revenue came in crypto; payments cleared instantly.

One afternoon, a major real-world brand contacted him: "We love your aesthetic. Would you design a limited virtual-wear drop for our NFT launch?" It was a moment of realization — the boundaries between real and virtual commerce had vanished.

Months later, Ethan attended a virtual fashion week in Decentraland. Standing on a glittering runway, his avatar watched holographic models display outfits he had once drawn in pencil. Fans cheered in digital chat bubbles. The host announced, "MetaThreadz just crossed one million in lifetime sales."

When he logged off that night, Ethan looked around his modest apartment and smiled. The rent, the bills, the old worries — all paid through pixels and code.

He whispered, "I sell imagination now."

The Metaverse had turned him from a struggling shopkeeper into a global merchant — proof that in this new economy, creativity was currency and belief was the only capital required to begin.

Chapter 5

Avatars, Identity & Self-Expression in the Metaverse

The Metaverse isn't only about technology and economics — it's about *identity*. In virtual worlds, who you appear to be and how you express yourself shape the way others interact with you, trust you, and do business with you. Your avatar is your digital mirror — part art, part psychology, and part brand.

1 — The Avatar as a Digital Self

In the Metaverse, you are represented by an avatar — a customized 3-D character that moves, speaks, and expresses emotion through gestures and voice. An avatar can look realistic, fantastical, or abstract. Some people replicate their real appearance; others create alter egos that reflect ambition, creativity, or a side of themselves that the physical world rarely sees.

Avatars serve as a psychological extension of self-image. Studies show that people often adopt behavior patterns matching their avatars — a phenomenon called *the Proteus Effect*. A confident-looking avatar can lead to more assertive communication and greater risk-taking in entrepreneurial settings.

2 — Identity and Ownership

Unlike traditional social media profiles, your Metaverse identity is not stored on a corporate server — it is verified through blockchain. Your digital clothing, name, and achievements are NFT assets that you truly own. This means your reputation and brand travel with you across platforms, allowing for a persistent and authentic digital presence.

Soon, a single decentralized identity will let you log in to any world instantly, carrying credentials, portfolios, and social proof. Think of it as a passport for the new internet.

3 — Fashion and Digital Self-Expression

Virtual fashion is booming. Luxury brands like Gucci and Nike now release exclusive wearables and NFT collections. In a world without physical constraints, creativity is limitless — people wear wings, armor, or glowing auras to project status and style.

This new fashion economy empowers independent designers to create their own labels without factories or inventory. Avatars become living billboards for artistic expression.

4 — Social and Psychological Impact

Identity in the Metaverse can liberate people from biases and limitations. Someone shy in real life might become a charismatic speaker as a digital host. Others use their avatars to explore gender, age, or culture dynamics in a safe environment. Yet this freedom also raises questions of authenticity and ethics — what happens when appearance can be infinitely edited?

Responsible participation requires balance: use avatars to express, not to deceive. The Metaverse thrives when creativity and trust coexist.

5 — Branding Your Digital Identity

Your avatar is your brand. Professionals are already building recognizable personas — consultants with signature color schemes, educators with distinct outfits, and creators whose avatars act as mascots for their businesses.

To establish a memorable digital identity:

- Keep a consistent look across platforms.
- Create a unique voice and communication style.
- Use NFT badges or collectibles as credentials of trust.

- Link your avatar to your real-world values and mission.

6 — The Evolution of Identity

In the future, avatars will grow more intelligent through AI integration. Your digital twin could attend meetings for you, speak in your voice, and remember your preferences. Identity will become fluid — a collaboration between you and your digital counterpart.

The Metaverse is not erasing who we are; it is *amplifying* us. It gives humans a chance to reinvent themselves without leaving their integrity behind.

Your avatar is your ambassador to infinite worlds — make it count.

"Becoming Nova"

Sofia was a graphic designer by day and an introvert by nature. Public speaking terrified her, and networking events left her drained. One evening, a friend invited her to a Metaverse conference for digital creatives. "Just log in," he said. "No pressure — you don't even have to show your face."

She downloaded the app and spent hours crafting her avatar. She named her *Nova* — a futuristic version of herself with silver hair, luminescent eyes, and a sleek digital suit lined with blue light. It was bolder and braver than she had ever felt.

When she entered the conference hall, avatars from every corner of the world floated around animated booths. Music played softly as hosts presented their NFT collections on giant screens. At first, Sofia hid in the corner, listening. But then someone complimented Nova's design. "Your jacket is amazing! Did you make it yourself?"

Sofia smiled. "Yes, I did."

That simple exchange sparked a conversation that lasted an hour. Nova was everything Sofia wished she could be — confident, creative, unapologetic. Within weeks, she was hosting her own virtual gallery tours showcasing digital art. Her following grew. Brands approached her to design avatars for their staff. In Zoom meetings, clients started calling her Nova even offline.

At first, Sofia worried she was living two lives. But she soon realized that Nova was not a mask — she was a mirror. The Metaverse had given Sofia a safe space to discover her authentic voice. Through digital expression, she had found real-world confidence.

Months later, she stood on a virtual stage before hundreds of avatars at a design summit. Her voice echoed through the hall. "Your avatar isn't a costume," she said. "It's a canvas. Use it to paint the person you want to become."

When the applause filled her headset, Sofia removed it and looked at her reflection on the screen. The woman staring back smiled — not as Sofia the designer, but as Nova the creator who had bridged two worlds.

Chapter 6

Social Life & Community Building in the Metaverse

The beating heart of the Metaverse isn't technology — it's *community.* Every digital world thrives or fails based on how well people connect, collaborate, and create shared meaning inside it. While the code provides structure, the people provide soul.

1 — The New Digital Society

The Metaverse is rapidly becoming the social layer of Web 3.0. It's not limited to games or entertainment — it's where friendships, businesses, education, and even activism take shape. Users gather in virtual cafés, attend concerts, host conferences, and celebrate birthdays together — all through avatars.

These spaces foster a sense of belonging that traditional social media often lacks. In the Metaverse, you don't just *watch* others live — you *live alongside them.*

2 — Building Communities That Matter

A thriving virtual community shares three key elements:

1. **Shared Purpose:** Whether it's art, gaming, wellness, or entrepreneurship, people unite around common values.

2. **Engagement:** Events, challenges, and co-creation keep members active.

3. **Governance:** Many communities use *DAOs* (Decentralized Autonomous Organizations) to make collective decisions. DAO members vote on proposals, budgets, and project direction using blockchain-based tokens, creating transparent and democratic leadership.

Strong communities start with a clear "why." In the Metaverse, authenticity and contribution attract more followers than flashy graphics ever will.

3 — Communication and Interaction

Voice chat, motion tracking, and AI translation now enable realistic interaction between users worldwide. A conversation between avatars can feel as genuine as an in-person exchange. You can shake hands, dance, share emojis, or collaborate on building a project in real time.

Virtual events like *Metaverse Fashion Week* or *VR EduSummit* show how global participation transcends geography. These moments build trust, empathy, and partnership — the same foundations of human society, just re-coded for the digital age.

4 — Networking and Collaboration

The Metaverse flattens hierarchies. You might find yourself standing next to a CEO, an artist, and a student — all equal within the same digital space. Collaboration happens organically: someone might invite you to design a virtual storefront, teach a class, or co-host an NFT drop.

Communities that support skill-sharing and mentorship grow the fastest. People don't just log in for entertainment; they log in to learn, contribute, and belong.

5 — Challenges of Digital Society

As with any society, challenges exist: harassment, misinformation, and exclusion can occur if moderation tools are weak. Responsible communities create codes of conduct, identity verification options, and positive reinforcement systems that reward kindness and collaboration.

Balance is crucial. The Metaverse is immersive, but it shouldn't replace real-world connection — it should enhance it.

6 — The Future of Connection

Within the next decade, virtual communities will rival physical cities in scale and diversity. Virtual nations, professional guilds, and decentralized schools will redefine how humans organize. The best leaders will be those who understand both the emotional and technical sides of digital society.

The future belongs to *community builders* — those who can gather people around a mission and inspire them to co-create value that transcends borders and platforms.

In the Metaverse, connection is currency — and collaboration is power.

"The City of Light"

When Marcus first logged into *Luma City*, it was nearly empty — a vast neon landscape of towers waiting for people to give it purpose. The developers had invited early users to "build something meaningful." Most ignored it. But Marcus, a lifelong teacher and volunteer, saw an opportunity.

He created a small plaza with benches, digital trees, and a sign that read: *"Community Hub — Helping New Users Navigate the Metaverse."* He spent hours greeting strangers, answering questions, and guiding them through their first steps. Slowly, visitors started returning. Some brought friends. Others offered to help.

A musician added a stage; an artist built a gallery; a coder created a vending machine that dispensed free NFT gifts for newcomers. The plaza became a meeting point for creators from around the world.

Marcus scheduled weekly "Build Nights," where volunteers constructed new areas together. One week they built a meditation garden; the next, a mentorship center for young designers. The hub evolved from a simple plaza into a thriving virtual neighborhood known as the *City of Light*.

As attendance grew, Marcus realized his project had become a DAO. Members voted on new expansions and contributed crypto donations to maintain servers. Leadership was decentralized; everyone had a voice.

One evening, a young woman from Argentina messaged him privately: "I was struggling with depression before I found this place. Building here gave me purpose again. Thank you."

Marcus stared at the message for a long moment. He had spent his career teaching in classrooms of thirty students, but here, in this borderless city of avatars, he had reached thousands.

When he logged in that weekend, fireworks filled the digital sky — a surprise organized by the community to celebrate the hub's one-year anniversary. As the glowing lights reflected off the avatar faces around him, Marcus realized something profound: the Metaverse wasn't just pixels or code. It was *people* — connected by curiosity, kindness, and a shared dream of belonging.

He removed his headset later that night, eyes still shimmering from the glow of Luma City, and whispered, "Humanity didn't disappear into the Metaverse — it rediscovered itself there."

Chapter 7

The Role of Big Tech & Decentralization in Shaping the Metaverse

The Metaverse is being built on two opposing yet interconnected forces: **corporate centralization** and **decentralized innovation**. Understanding the tension between them is vital to predicting how this digital universe will evolve — and how individuals can keep control of their data, identity, and creative power.

1 — The Corporate Vision of the Metaverse

Tech giants such as **Meta (Facebook)**, **Microsoft**, **Apple**, and **Google** have invested billions to construct proprietary virtual ecosystems. Their goal is to merge hardware, software, and commerce into closed networks that dominate user engagement — much like social-media platforms did in Web 2.0.

Meta's "Horizon Worlds," Microsoft's "Mesh," and Apple's Vision Pro ecosystem illustrate this strategy: seamless user experiences tied to centralized data collection and subscription models. These corporations aim to onboard billions quickly — but at the cost of user sovereignty.

2 — The Decentralized Alternative

In contrast, projects such as **Decentraland**, **The Sandbox**, **Somnium Space**, and **Spatial** operate on blockchain networks. They promote *user ownership* of land, assets, and governance rights through **NFTs** and **DAOs**. These communities believe the Metaverse should belong to its citizens, not to a handful of companies.

Decentralization ensures transparency and portability. If one platform fails, your digital assets remain verifiable on-chain and usable elsewhere — a protection impossible in closed systems.

3 — Data, Privacy & Ownership

Centralized platforms profit from user data; decentralized ones empower users to monetize or withhold it. In a blockchain-based Metaverse, you decide what to share. Smart-contract wallets replace invasive ad tracking, and verified anonymity becomes possible.

Still, decentralization introduces challenges — from security flaws to user responsibility. Without a central authority, you become your own bank and guardian of your assets. Losing a private key can mean losing an entire identity.

4 — Interoperability: Bridging the Divide

The future likely lies in **hybrid integration** — where corporate infrastructure provides scale and polish while open-source protocols maintain freedom and mobility. Standards bodies such as the Open Metaverse Alliance (OMA3) and Metaverse Standards Forum are already developing interoperability frameworks.

Eventually, you might wear an Apple headset to explore a world built by an independent DAO, using a wallet verified on Ethereum and powered by cloud servers from Google Cloud. True progress requires cooperation between giants and innovators alike.

5 — Economic Influence and Control

Corporations bring capital, advertising power, and mainstream adoption. Start-ups and DAOs bring creativity, inclusion, and agility. The healthiest ecosystem will balance both — allowing enterprise-grade infrastructure to coexist with grassroots experimentation.

If decentralization wins entirely, scalability may suffer; if corporations dominate, freedom will shrink. The equilibrium defines the moral architecture of the future internet.

6 — What This Means for You

As a creator or investor, understanding this balance helps you make strategic choices:

- **Diversify** — participate in both corporate and decentralized worlds.
- **Own your identity** — keep assets in your own wallet, not inside a platform.
- **Advocate for open standards** — support projects that protect user rights.

The future Metaverse will be built by millions of contributors, not a single company. The power struggle between centralization and decentralization isn't a battle to fear — it's a negotiation that will define digital freedom for generations.

"The Two Worlds"

Lara had spent ten years climbing the ladder at a major tech conglomerate, helping design the user-interface for its new Metaverse headset. Every meeting buzzed with ambition — the CEO dreamed aloud of a world where billions would log in daily, surrounded by company-owned experiences.

She admired the sleekness of it all — but something felt wrong. Every prototype required a corporate login; every "free" avatar skin came with data-collection terms buried in legal text. The Metaverse they were building looked beautiful — yet it was a gilded cage.

One night after work, Lara joined a decentralized community event inside The Sandbox. The graphics were simpler, the code a bit clunky — but the atmosphere was electric. Musicians streamed live, builders traded NFTs, and volunteers voted on next week's upgrades. No executives, no permissions — just creation.

She struck up a conversation with an avatar named *CodeMason*. He ran a DAO that funded open-source VR tools. "Here," he said, sending her a link, "you can help us design the next cross-world teleportation protocol."

Lara laughed. "You're inviting a corporate designer to your rebel alliance?"

"Why not?" he said. "We need both worlds — your structure, our freedom."

Weeks turned into months. By day she optimized corporate user flows; by night she built bridges for decentralized explorers. Eventually her two worlds collided. Her company announced a partnership with the very DAO she'd been volunteering for. They wanted interoperability — the same concept she'd been advocating in secret.

During the first joint demo, users seamlessly jumped from the corporate world into the decentralized city without losing avatars or assets. The chat exploded with excitement: *"It works!"*

After the event, Lara stood on a virtual balcony overlooking the merging skylines — one polished and corporate, the other raw and community-built. "This," she thought, "is what the future should look like — not walls, but windows."

She realized the Metaverse didn't have to be a war between giants and dreamers. It could be a collaboration — a network where power and participation finally shared the same stage.

Removing her headset, she smiled. "Two worlds," she whispered, "but one future."

Chapter 8

The Metaverse and Education: Learning Without Borders

Education is one of the Metaverse's most transformative frontiers. Beyond entertainment and commerce, it promises to redefine *how* people learn — not through screens and slides, but through full-bodied experience. A student can now walk through ancient Rome, explore the solar system, or perform a virtual surgery — all from a living room.

1 — From Online Learning to Immersive Learning

Traditional e-learning (Zoom calls, PDFs, pre-recorded videos) struggles to keep attention. The Metaverse replaces passive consumption with **experiential learning**. Learners become *participants* in dynamic simulations, able to interact, explore, and collaborate in 3-D.

Imagine studying marine biology by diving into a coral reef with your classmates or practicing public speaking before an audience of responsive avatars. Memory retention and engagement skyrocket because the experience is *felt*, not just read.

2 — The Anatomy of a Virtual Classroom

A Metaverse classroom combines several technologies:

- **3-D environments** built with Unity or Unreal Engine to replicate real or imaginary spaces.
- **Avatars** representing teachers and students, creating a sense of presence and equality.
- **Interactive objects** that respond to voice or movement, turning lessons into games.
- **AI tutors** that adapt difficulty and pacing based on each learner's progress.
- **Blockchain certification** that issues verifiable credentials (NFT diplomas or skill badges).

These elements together foster *participation, collaboration,* and *proof of learning*.

3 — Global Accessibility and Inclusion

In the Metaverse, geography disappears. A student in Kenya can attend a physics lecture hosted in London alongside peers from Brazil and Japan. Language barriers fade through instant AI translation. The cost of entry continues to drop as headsets become cheaper and browser-based access expands.

For marginalized or remote communities, this means opportunity. No travel visas, no expensive dorms — just curiosity and connectivity.

4 — The New Role of Educators

Teachers evolve from lecturers into **experience designers**. Their task is not merely to deliver facts but to craft worlds that make knowledge tangible. A history teacher might recreate the signing of the Declaration of Independence; a chemistry instructor might build a molecular playground where atoms dance and combine in real time.

Educators also gain global reach. One talented teacher can now instruct thousands through immersive courses that generate passive income as perpetual digital assets.

5 — Institutional Adoption and Corporate Training

Universities like Stanford, MIT, and Seoul University have already launched VR classrooms. Fortune 500 companies train employees in virtual simulations for safety, sales, and leadership development. Walmart, for example, uses VR to prepare staff for Black Friday rushes.

Corporate training in the Metaverse reduces costs, accelerates learning, and provides real-time analytics on employee performance.

6 — Challenges and the Road Ahead

Adoption faces obstacles: hardware cost, bandwidth demands, and motion-sickness issues for some users. More importantly, accreditation and data privacy frameworks must evolve to ensure fairness and legitimacy.

Yet the direction is inevitable. As AI, AR, and blockchain converge, education will become borderless, adaptive, and deeply human again — because it restores curiosity and play to learning.

The Metaverse turns classrooms into universes, teachers into creators, and students into explorers.

"The Global Classroom"

The morning bell didn't ring anymore — it shimmered. A gentle chime echoed through Aisha's headset as she logged in from her small apartment in Nairobi. Her uniform wasn't fabric but code — a digital blazer stitched with her school's crest. With one click, the world unfolded around her: a floating island above clouds, where hundreds of students gathered on transparent platforms.

"Welcome, everyone," said Professor Lin, appearing as a friendly hologram. Behind him, the sky morphed into the solar system. Planets rotated slowly, glowing with detail. "Today, we'll be visiting Mars."

Aisha gasped as the ground shifted beneath her. In seconds, she stood on a red desert, wind brushing her avatar's suit. Dust devils swirled around robotic rovers. "Please form groups of three," said Lin. "Collect mineral samples using your scanners."

Her classmates — Pedro from Brazil and Amira from Egypt — waved through their headsets. They laughed as they searched for glowing stones, their voices clear despite oceans between them.

After class, Aisha attended an entrepreneurship workshop led by a guest speaker from Silicon Valley. He walked them through building a business model using interactive holograms. Each student designed a prototype product and presented it to a virtual panel for feedback.

Later, she entered a quiet garden — her school's reflection space — where AI mentors appeared to discuss her goals. "You've shown strong leadership," the AI said gently. "Would you like to join the global sustainability challenge next week?"

Aisha smiled. "Yes, please."

That evening, she took off her headset and looked around her room — small, dimly lit, but filled with possibility. She realized she'd spent the day traveling from Nairobi to Mars to California, meeting friends worldwide, learning skills that would change her life — all without leaving home.

The next morning, she woke up early, excited for history class. Today they would visit ancient Egypt — her favorite lesson. As she slipped the headset back on, she whispered, "The world isn't far away anymore."

In that moment, Aisha understood the promise of the Metaverse: *knowledge without borders, and opportunity without permission.*

Chapter 9

Entertainment, Art & Creativity in the Metaverse

Entertainment has always driven technological revolutions — radio popularized storytelling, television reshaped culture, and the internet democratized creation. Now, the Metaverse is redefining entertainment once again. In this new dimension, **art, music, film, gaming, and live events** collide into interactive experiences people can explore, personalize, and even co-create.

1 — The Evolution of Digital Entertainment

The Metaverse builds on decades of digital creativity, but it upgrades everything by adding **presence**. Instead of watching a concert on a screen, you stand in the crowd. Instead of viewing an art piece, you walk around it. Instead of playing a game, you *live inside it*.

This transition from 2-D consumption to 3-D immersion shifts the audience from passive spectators to active participants.

2 — Virtual Concerts & Live Events

Major artists have already performed inside virtual worlds,

attracting millions:

- **Travis Scott** in Fortnite
- **Ariana Grande** in Rift Tour
- **Justin Bieber** in WaveXR
- Electronic DJs hosting weekly shows in Decentraland and VRChat

These events combine motion capture, holographic effects, and blockchain ticketing to create concerts impossible in the physical world — floating stages, gravity shifts, giant avatars, real-time animation effects.

Why Artists Love It:

- No venue fees
- Global audiences
- Digital merchandise sales (NFTs)
- Evergreen replay value

Virtual events will soon include film premieres, comedy shows, fitness classes, and even fashion runways where clothing can be purchased instantly as wearable NFTs.

3 — The Rise of Metaverse Art

Artists can now create **3-D sculptures, animated environments, living paintings, holographic galleries, and interactive installations.** These pieces are not limited by physics—art can defy gravity, change with time, or react to the viewer.

NFTs Transform the Art World:

- Artists retain royalties on resales
- Buyers receive verifiable proof of ownership
- Galleries can operate 24/7
- No shipping or physical storage

Virtual museums attract thousands. Entire careers now flourish exclusively in digital worlds.

4 — Gaming and Interactivity

Gaming is the backbone of Metaverse entertainment. But unlike traditional games, these worlds are:

- **Persistent** (they continue even when you log off)
- **Social** (millions interact simultaneously)

- **Economically driven** (players earn real currency through gameplay)

Play-to-earn titles let users earn tokens by completing quests, customizing avatars, or participating in world-building tasks.

5 — Film, Animation, and Storytelling

Filmmakers now use virtual worlds as both studios and stages. Movies can be shot entirely in VR using digital cameras that move through 3-D environments. Fans can later *step inside scenes* to explore them interactively.

Future storytelling will be:

- **Nonlinear**
- **Explorable**
- **Customizable**
- **Collaborative**

Imagine watching a mystery movie where you can walk around the crime scene yourself.

6 — Creativity Tools for Everyone

The Metaverse lowers the barrier to creation:

- No need for expensive cameras
- No need for physical materials
- Intuitive drag-and-drop design tools
- AI that generates music, landscapes, or 3-D models in seconds

Anyone — adult or child — can create worlds, stories, games, or art without technical expertise. Creativity becomes democratized.

7 — Economic Opportunities for Creators

Creators earn money through:

- NFT art drops
- Selling wearables
- Designing environments
- Producing events
- Licensing music or animation
- Operating virtual galleries
- Running metaverse film studios

- Selling game assets

Unlike traditional entertainment industries, the Metaverse lets creators keep ownership and revenue.

8 — Challenges Ahead

Intellectual property theft, copyright issues, and market speculation create risks. Creators must understand smart contracts, copyright tokens, and platform policies.

Still, the opportunity outweighs the challenges. The Metaverse is the greatest artistic frontier since the birth of the internet — a universe where creativity isn't just displayed... it's *felt.*

"The Artist Who Painted with Light"

Elena had spent years painting in her small Brooklyn studio, surrounded by canvases stacked like memories against the walls. She dreamed of showing her art to the world but lacked connections, gallery representation, and the confidence to pitch her work.

One night, while scrolling online, she clicked into a live tour of a virtual gallery hosted in Decentraland. The walls glowed with animated artwork that pulsed gently to ambient music. Guests from dozens of countries floated through the space, discussing color, movement, and meaning. Something inside Elena sparked. “What if I could put *my* art here?” she whispered.

That week, she learned to mint NFTs. She converted one of her canvases — a painting of a rising phoenix — into an animated version. With a trembling hand, she uploaded it into a small corner booth in a public gallery space.

Two days later, a message appeared: **“Your artwork has sold for 1.8 ETH.”**

Elena stared at the screen. She had never sold a physical painting for even half that amount.

Encouraged, she began creating exclusively for the Metaverse. She painted with light instead of oils — luminous colors that rippled like water. She created sculptures that defied gravity, twisting upward in fractal spirals. She built chambers where music triggered shifting patterns across the walls.

Soon, she opened *The Phoenix Room* — her own virtual gallery. Visitors entered through a portal of flames that dissolved into a star-lit hall. Avatars walked slowly, mesmerized, as her pieces responded to their footsteps, pulsing with warmth.

One evening, she hosted her first live exhibition. Hundreds of avatars gathered. Elena, represented by a glowing gold avatar, floated above the crowd and said:

"Thank you for being here. I couldn't afford a real-world gallery. But here, I can build one as big as my imagination."

As she toured the visitors through each artwork, people typed emotional comments in the chat. A woman from South Korea said Elena's piece reminded her of her late mother. A young man from Nigeria said her use of color inspired him to start drawing again. For the first time, Elena felt seen across continents.

After the event, a director from a virtual film studio messaged her: **"Your art feels alive. Would you like to collaborate on an immersive movie?"**

Elena's breath caught. She had spent years creating alone in silence... and now her work lived in a world without walls.

That night, she took off her headset, tears welling. The studio was still small, the canvases still stacked — but everything had changed.

In the Metaverse, she wasn't limited by rent prices, gallery politics, or geographical boundaries. She was an artist unbound — painting dreams across a universe of infinite light.

Chapter 10

The Future of the Metaverse: Opportunities, Risks & Predictions

The Metaverse is still in its early stages — comparable to the internet around 1995. Many people have heard of it, but few understand its potential. Some dismiss it as a fad; others believe it will reshape society. The truth lies somewhere in between: the Metaverse is not a single destination, but a long-term evolution of how humans live, work, create, and connect online.

This chapter explores where the Metaverse is heading, the industries it will transform, and the opportunities and risks early adopters must navigate.

1 — The Next Evolution of the Internet

Over the next decade, the Metaverse will mature into a fully integrated layer of the internet. Instead of websites, we will enter *spaces.* Instead of apps, we will interact with *environments.* Instead of profiles, we will present *avatars and digital identities.*

The line between online and offline will blur, creating a hybrid reality where immersive digital experiences complement physical life.

Key features of this evolution:

- **Spatial web navigation** (you walk through the internet instead of scrolling)
- **3-D social environments**
- **Persistent digital economies**
- **AI-powered assistants and avatars**
- **Wearable devices replacing smartphones**

The future internet will be immersive, portable, decentralized, and intelligent.

2 — Industries That Will Be Transformed

The Metaverse will impact every major sector:

a. Work & Careers

Remote work becomes immersive offices, virtual campuses, AI-powered assistants, and cross-border collaboration.

b. Education

Virtual classrooms, global learning platforms, simulation-based training, AI tutors, and blockchain credentials will redefine learning.

c. Real Estate & Architecture

Digital property markets grow as architects design virtual cities, stores, schools, and entertainment districts.

d. Healthcare

VR therapy, remote diagnostics, and surgical training simulations become normal.

e. Retail & Fashion

Virtual stores, digital clothing, and interactive product experiences dominate.

f. Gaming & Entertainment

Games become worlds, movies become explorable, concerts become experiences, and creators become global brands.

g. Finance

Crypto, DeFi, tokenized assets, and digital banking power the underlying economy.

Every industry will either adapt or be replaced by Metaverse-native competitors.

3 — The Rise of AI and Autonomous Worlds

AI will transform the Metaverse from static landscapes into living ecosystems. Worlds will grow and evolve without human input. AI characters will become indistinguishable from real users. AI builders will design environments autonomously.

AI + Metaverse =

- dynamic storytelling
- intelligent NPCs
- personalized environments
- real-time translation
- procedural content generation
- AI clones of real people for customer service, entertainment, or education

The Metaverse becomes an adaptive universe — intelligent, personalized, and limitless.

4 — Predictions for the Next 10–20 Years

1. **One billion people will use some form of Metaverse platform.**
2. **Digital identity will become as important as physical identity.**
3. **Virtual offices will replace many corporate headquarters.**
4. **AI-generated worlds will appear faster than humans can explore them.**
5. **Governments will regulate virtual property, identity theft, crypto assets, and digital rights.**
6. **Entire professions will emerge:**
    - virtual architects
    - avatar stylists
    - AI-world storytellers
    - virtual-city civil engineers
    - digital real-estate agents
    - Metaverse teachers & tour guides

7. **Digital wealth will rival physical wealth**, with tokenized assets, passive-income worlds, and global digital businesses.

8. **Brain-computer interfaces** will eventually allow direct neural interaction with virtual space.

The Metaverse is not a trend — it is an economic and cultural shift.

5 — Risks & Challenges

While the potential is enormous, the Metaverse carries serious risks:

- **Privacy concerns** from sensors, biometrics, and behavioral tracking
- **Addiction and over-immersion**
- **Asset theft and hacking**
- **Speculative bubbles in virtual real estate**
- **Corporate monopolies controlling identity and access**
- **Regulation unclear or inconsistent**
- **Technological inequality**

- **Mental health risks** without moderation

Future leaders must balance innovation with ethical responsibility.

6 — The Opportunity for Early Adopters

Today's Metaverse pioneers will become tomorrow's digital landowners, creators, educators, architects, investors, and innovators.

To position yourself:

- Learn the platforms
- Build your identity
- Create digital assets
- Start offering services
- Join DAOs & communities
- Invest strategically
- Embrace both AI and Web3 tools

The Metaverse isn't something you wait for — it's something you *build.*

The future belongs to those who participate early, learn relentlessly, and innovate boldly.

This is your chance to stand at the beginning of a new era — and help shape it.

"The City That Didn't Exist Yet"

Aria stood on the balcony of her penthouse — not in New York or Dubai, but in a city that had no name yet. The skyline was still under construction, shimmering with floating cranes and beams of light. She watched as giant holographic trees grew pixel by pixel, planted by an AI she helped design.

Three years earlier, none of this existed. It was a blank space — an empty digital canvas. But Aria had a vision: a city built not by governments or corporations, but by its citizens.

She called it **Luminara**.

At first, only a few avatars roamed the empty streets. Aria spent hours designing the foundational districts — a creative hub, a learning center, and a marketplace. She invited architects, artists, musicians, and educators. She gave them free plots of land and told them one rule:

"Build something that makes someone's life better."

They did.

A musician built a symphony dome where sound waves turned into colors. A historian built a time-travel museum where visitors could walk through ancient civilizations. A teacher built a floating school where classrooms revolved around the planet like satellites.

As word spread, thousands arrived. They brought ideas, businesses, and dreams from every corner of Earth. Soon, Luminara needed governance. But instead of electing a mayor, they created a DAO. Every resident held a vote. AI moderated discussions. Decisions were transparent.

The city grew — beautifully, chaotically, organically.

One evening, Aria walked through the innovation district. A young student approached her — a small avatar with glowing eyes.

"Miss Aria, I built something," he said nervously.

He led her into a shimmering tunnel. At the end was a star-shaped capsule floating in mid-air.

"It's a memory vault," he explained. "A place where people can store moments from real life... then step back into them whenever they want."

Aria stepped inside. Holographic images flickered — a beach, a grandmother's smile, a child's first steps. The emotions felt real, warm, overwhelming.

When she stepped out, she wiped a tear. "You're going to help millions of people," she said.

Years passed. Luminara became a global phenomenon — a model of what virtual civilizations could become. Cities around the world studied its governance, its economic system, and its creativity engine powered by AI.

One night, standing again on her balcony, Aria looked out at the glowing city that stretched infinitely across the digital horizon.

This world was no longer a place people *escaped* to. It was a place they *grew* in. A place where ideas became architecture, dreams became economies, and strangers became citizens.

She whispered, "The future isn't coming... it's already here."

And for the first time, she understood:

The Metaverse wasn't just the next Internet. It was the next *civilization*.

Final Thoughts

The Metaverse is no longer a distant concept reserved for futurists or technologists — it is rapidly becoming a reality that will transform how humanity communicates, learns, creates, works, and builds wealth. Throughout this book, you've taken your first step into understanding a world where imagination becomes architecture, where identity becomes self-designed, and where opportunity is no longer constrained by geography, education, or privilege. You've seen how virtual worlds are built, how economies arise from digital scarcity, how avatars become extensions of identity, and how new careers and industries are already emerging. You've witnessed storytellers, artists, teachers, and entrepreneurs reinvent themselves in virtual universes that feel as real as any physical city. And you've glimpsed a future where the next generation will learn in immersive classrooms, socialize in interactive 3-D spaces, and build wealth through digital ownership that transcends borders.

Yet despite all the advancements and promises, the Metaverse is still in its infancy. We are early. The infrastructure is being laid, the standards are being debated, the platforms are competing, and the rules of digital citizenship are being formed. Early adopters like you have the rare opportunity to shape this frontier — to influence how ownership works, how communities govern themselves, how creative assets are protected, and how AI coexists with human imagination. The next decade will not be defined by a single company or technology but by millions of users contributing ideas, inventions, businesses, and art that blur the boundaries between reality and possibility.

The truth is that the Metaverse is not just a technological shift — it is a cultural shift. It forces us to rethink identity, challenge traditional education, redefine careers, and imagine new pathways for financial independence. It urges us to ask deeper questions: Who do we want to become when limits fade? What kind of society do we want to build? How can we design digital worlds that are safe, inclusive, ethical, and empowering for all? These questions matter because our virtual environments will shape human behavior just as strongly as our physical ones do.

The Metaverse will also require responsibility. With decentralized ownership comes personal accountability. With digital freedom comes the need for digital literacy. With immersive experiences comes the obligation to maintain balance between virtual life and physical well-being. With global access comes the challenge of ensuring equity so that the opportunities of the Metaverse don't become another divide between the connected and the disconnected. The pioneers of this new era — creators, educators, investors, developers, and visionaries — must commit to building with intention, empathy, and foresight.

But above all, the Metaverse represents hope. It offers the dream of a world where creativity is currency, where education is accessible to all, where identity is fluid and self-determined, where careers emerge from passion, and where borders dissolve into global collaboration. It offers every person — regardless of where they were born — the chance to participate in a global economy fueled by innovation and imagination. For many, it will unlock opportunities that were previously unthinkable: launching digital businesses with no overhead, selling art without galleries, teaching students worldwide from a small apartment, or building virtual architecture seen by millions.

As we conclude this book, remember one truth: the Metaverse is not something you wait for — it is something you build. Every world, every tool, every avatar, every marketplace, and every DAO is created by people like you. Your curiosity, your experiments, your ideas, and your willingness to learn are the seeds that will grow into the next generation of digital worlds. Whether you become a creator, investor, educator, storyteller, developer, or explorer, your contribution matters more than you realize. This is not science fiction — it is the beginning of a new digital civilization.

You now stand at the threshold of the greatest technological transformation since the birth of the internet. You have the knowledge, the perspective, and the imagination to participate in it. As you continue your journey, I encourage you to explore boldly, experiment fearlessly, and create unapologetically. The Metaverse belongs to the builders, the dreamers, the risk-takers, and the pioneers who see opportunity where others see uncertainty. Welcome to the next chapter of human evolution. The future is not coming — it is already here, and you are now part of it.

www.ingramcontent.com/pod-product-compliance
Ingram Content Group UK Ltd.
Pitfield, Milton Keynes, MK11 3LW, UK
UKHW020156290926
15471UKWH00005B/897

9 798295 491047